50 Raw Vegan Sushi Roll Recipes for Home

By: Kelly Johnson

Table of Contents

- Avocado and cucumber rolls
- Mango and red pepper rolls
- Carrot and avocado rolls
- Spicy cauliflower rolls
- Beet and avocado rolls
- Asparagus and bell pepper rolls
- Zucchini and mushroom rolls
- Sweet potato and avocado rolls
- Cucumber and radish rolls
- Spinach and sun-dried tomato rolls
- Watermelon and cucumber rolls
- Pineapple and bell pepper rolls
- Jicama and mango rolls
- Coconut and avocado rolls
- Portobello mushroom and spinach rolls
- Bell pepper and avocado rolls
- Sweet potato and kale rolls
- Cauliflower rice and avocado rolls
- Sunflower seed pate and cucumber rolls
- Kimchi and avocado rolls
- Nori-wrapped vegetable sticks with almond butter
- Cucumber and quinoa rolls
- Tomato and basil rolls
- Broccoli and carrot rolls
- Radish and avocado rolls
- Mango and jalapeño rolls
- Asparagus and avocado rolls
- Bell pepper and jicama rolls
- Spinach and avocado rolls
- Cabbage and carrot rolls
- Sesame marinated tofu rolls
- Smoked tofu and cucumber rolls
- Pickled ginger and avocado rolls
- Spicy cashew cheese and bell pepper rolls
- Lentil and carrot rolls

- Kimchi and cauliflower rice rolls
- Beet and spinach rolls
- Cucumber and mango rolls
- Cauliflower rice and avocado rolls with sesame seeds
- Red cabbage and carrot rolls
- Sunflower seed pate and cucumber rolls
- Portobello mushroom and avocado rolls
- Mango and red cabbage rolls
- Spinach and bell pepper rolls
- Sweet potato and cucumber rolls
- Beet and apple rolls
- Mango and avocado rolls with cilantro
- Carrot and sunflower seed pate rolls
- Cucumber and marinated tofu rolls
- Avocado and bell pepper rolls

Avocado and cucumber rolls

Ingredients:

- 2 cups sushi rice
- 2 1/2 cups water
- 1/3 cup rice vinegar
- 2 tablespoons sugar
- 1 teaspoon salt
- 2 ripe avocados, sliced
- 1 large cucumber, julienned
- 4 sheets nori (seaweed)
- Soy sauce, for serving
- Wasabi, for serving
- Pickled ginger, for serving

Instructions:

Prepare the Rice:
- Rinse the sushi rice in a fine-mesh strainer under cold water until the water runs clear.
- Combine the rinsed rice and water in a rice cooker or pot and cook according to the manufacturer's instructions.
- Once cooked, transfer the rice to a large bowl and let it cool slightly.

Make the Sushi Rice Seasoning:
- In a small saucepan, combine the rice vinegar, sugar, and salt.
- Heat over low heat, stirring until the sugar and salt dissolve.
- Pour the vinegar mixture over the cooked rice and gently fold it in until well combined. Let the rice cool completely.

Prepare the Ingredients:
- Slice the avocado and julienne the cucumber into long, thin strips.

Assemble the Rolls:
- Place a sheet of nori on a bamboo sushi rolling mat with the shiny side facing down.
- With wet hands, spread a thin layer of sushi rice evenly over the nori, leaving about a 1-inch border at the top edge.
- Arrange slices of avocado and cucumber in a line across the center of the rice.

Roll the Sushi:

- Starting from the bottom edge, tightly roll the sushi using the bamboo mat, applying gentle pressure as you roll.
- Wet the top border of the nori with water to seal the roll.
- Continue rolling until the entire nori sheet is rolled up.

Slice and Serve:
- Use a sharp knife to slice the roll into 6-8 pieces.
- Repeat the process with the remaining ingredients.
- Serve the avocado and cucumber rolls with soy sauce, wasabi, and pickled ginger on the side.

Enjoy your homemade avocado and cucumber sushi rolls! They make a refreshing and healthy snack or meal option.

Mango and red pepper rolls

Ingredients:

- 2 cups sushi rice
- 2 1/2 cups water
- 1/3 cup rice vinegar
- 2 tablespoons sugar
- 1 teaspoon salt
- 1 ripe mango, peeled and thinly sliced
- 1 red bell pepper, thinly sliced
- 4 sheets nori (seaweed)
- Soy sauce, for serving
- Wasabi, for serving
- Pickled ginger, for serving

Instructions:

Prepare the Rice:
- Rinse the sushi rice in a fine-mesh strainer under cold water until the water runs clear.
- Combine the rinsed rice and water in a rice cooker or pot and cook according to the manufacturer's instructions.
- Once cooked, transfer the rice to a large bowl and let it cool slightly.

Make the Sushi Rice Seasoning:
- In a small saucepan, combine the rice vinegar, sugar, and salt.
- Heat over low heat, stirring until the sugar and salt dissolve.
- Pour the vinegar mixture over the cooked rice and gently fold it in until well combined. Let the rice cool completely.

Prepare the Ingredients:
- Peel the mango and thinly slice it.
- Thinly slice the red bell pepper.

Assemble the Rolls:
- Place a sheet of nori on a bamboo sushi rolling mat with the shiny side facing down.
- With wet hands, spread a thin layer of sushi rice evenly over the nori, leaving about a 1-inch border at the top edge.
- Arrange slices of mango and red bell pepper in a line across the center of the rice.

Roll the Sushi:

- Starting from the bottom edge, tightly roll the sushi using the bamboo mat, applying gentle pressure as you roll.
- Wet the top border of the nori with water to seal the roll.
- Continue rolling until the entire nori sheet is rolled up.

Slice and Serve:
- Use a sharp knife to slice the roll into 6-8 pieces.
- Repeat the process with the remaining ingredients.
- Serve the mango and red pepper rolls with soy sauce, wasabi, and pickled ginger on the side.

Enjoy your homemade mango and red pepper sushi rolls! They offer a delicious combination of flavors and make a perfect appetizer or light meal.

Carrot and avocado rolls

Ingredients:

- Nori seaweed sheets
- 1 ripe avocado
- 1 large carrot
- Sushi rice
- Rice vinegar
- Sugar
- Salt
- Soy sauce (for dipping, optional)
- Wasabi (for dipping, optional)
- Pickled ginger (for serving, optional)

Instructions:

Cook the sushi rice according to package instructions. Once cooked, season with a mixture of rice vinegar, sugar, and salt to taste. Allow the rice to cool to room temperature.
While the rice is cooking, prepare the vegetables. Peel the carrot and slice it into thin strips. Peel and slice the avocado into thin strips as well.
Lay a sheet of nori seaweed on a bamboo sushi rolling mat, shiny side down. Spread a thin layer of sushi rice evenly over the nori, leaving about an inch of space at the top edge.
Arrange the carrot and avocado strips horizontally across the center of the rice-covered nori sheet.
Using the bamboo mat, carefully roll the nori sheet tightly around the filling ingredients, applying gentle pressure as you roll to ensure a compact roll.
Once rolled, use a sharp knife to slice the roll into individual pieces, about 1 inch thick.
Serve the carrot and avocado rolls with soy sauce, wasabi, and pickled ginger on the side, if desired.

Enjoy your homemade carrot and avocado rolls!

Spicy cauliflower rolls

Ingredients:

- Nori seaweed sheets
- 1 small head of cauliflower
- 2 tablespoons soy sauce
- 1 tablespoon sriracha sauce (adjust to taste)
- 1 tablespoon rice vinegar
- 1 teaspoon sesame oil
- Sushi rice
- Sugar
- Salt
- Soy sauce (for dipping, optional)
- Wasabi (for dipping, optional)
- Pickled ginger (for serving, optional)

Instructions:

Preheat your oven to 400°F (200°C).
Break the cauliflower into small florets and place them on a baking sheet lined with parchment paper.
In a small bowl, mix together the soy sauce, sriracha sauce, rice vinegar, and sesame oil.
Pour the sauce mixture over the cauliflower florets and toss until evenly coated.
Roast the cauliflower in the preheated oven for about 20-25 minutes, or until tender and slightly caramelized.
While the cauliflower is roasting, prepare the sushi rice according to package instructions. Season the rice with a mixture of rice vinegar, sugar, and salt to taste. Allow the rice to cool to room temperature.
Lay a sheet of nori seaweed on a bamboo sushi rolling mat, shiny side down. Spread a thin layer of sushi rice evenly over the nori, leaving about an inch of space at the top edge.
Arrange the roasted cauliflower pieces horizontally across the center of the rice-covered nori sheet.
Using the bamboo mat, carefully roll the nori sheet tightly around the filling ingredients, applying gentle pressure as you roll to ensure a compact roll.

Once rolled, use a sharp knife to slice the roll into individual pieces, about 1 inch thick.
Serve the spicy cauliflower rolls with soy sauce, wasabi, and pickled ginger on the side, if desired.

Enjoy your homemade spicy cauliflower rolls!

Beet and avocado rolls

Ingredients:

- 2 large beets
- 1 ripe avocado
- 4-6 large lettuce leaves (such as romaine or butter lettuce)
- 1 tablespoon lemon juice
- Salt and pepper to taste
- Optional: sesame seeds or chopped nuts for garnish

Instructions:

Peel the beets and slice them thinly lengthwise using a mandoline slicer or a sharp knife. You want the slices to be thin enough to roll easily.

Steam or boil the beet slices until they are just tender, about 5-7 minutes. Be careful not to overcook them, as you want them to still be firm enough to roll.

While the beets are cooking, mash the avocado in a small bowl and season with lemon juice, salt, and pepper.

Lay out the lettuce leaves on a clean surface. Spread a thin layer of mashed avocado onto each leaf.

Once the beet slices are cooked, allow them to cool slightly. Place a few slices of beet on top of the mashed avocado on each lettuce leaf.

Carefully roll up each lettuce leaf, enclosing the beet and avocado filling inside.

If desired, sprinkle sesame seeds or chopped nuts on top of the rolls for added flavor and texture.

Serve the beet and avocado rolls immediately, or store them in the refrigerator for later. They make a great healthy snack or appetizer! Enjoy!

Asparagus and bell pepper rolls

Ingredients:

- 12 asparagus spears, tough ends trimmed
- 1 large red bell pepper, thinly sliced into strips
- 1 large yellow bell pepper, thinly sliced into strips
- 2 tablespoons olive oil
- 2 cloves garlic, minced
- Salt and pepper to taste
- Optional: Balsamic glaze or vinaigrette for drizzling

Instructions:

Preheat your oven to 400°F (200°C).
In a large bowl, toss the asparagus spears and bell pepper strips with olive oil, minced garlic, salt, and pepper until evenly coated.
Spread the vegetables out in a single layer on a baking sheet lined with parchment paper.
Roast the vegetables in the preheated oven for about 10-15 minutes, or until the asparagus is tender and the bell peppers are slightly caramelized.
Remove the vegetables from the oven and allow them to cool slightly.
To assemble the rolls, place a few asparagus spears and bell pepper strips on one end of each strip of bell pepper. Carefully roll up the bell pepper strip around the vegetables to form a tight roll.
Repeat with the remaining asparagus and bell pepper strips until all the vegetables are used.
If desired, drizzle the rolls with balsamic glaze or vinaigrette for added flavor.
Serve the asparagus and bell pepper rolls immediately, or refrigerate them for later. They make a delicious and colorful appetizer or side dish. Enjoy!

Zucchini and mushroom rolls

Ingredients:

- 2 medium zucchinis
- 8-10 large button mushrooms, stems removed
- 2 tablespoons olive oil
- 2 cloves garlic, minced
- 1 teaspoon dried thyme (or 1 tablespoon fresh thyme leaves)
- Salt and pepper to taste
- Toothpicks or small skewers

Instructions:

Preheat your oven to 375°F (190°C).
Using a mandoline slicer or a sharp knife, slice the zucchinis lengthwise into thin strips, about 1/8 inch thick.
In a small bowl, whisk together the olive oil, minced garlic, dried thyme, salt, and pepper.
Brush both sides of each zucchini strip with the olive oil mixture.
Place a mushroom at one end of each zucchini strip and roll it up tightly.
Secure each roll with a toothpick or small skewer to prevent it from unraveling.
Place the zucchini and mushroom rolls on a baking sheet lined with parchment paper, seam side down.
Bake in the preheated oven for 15-20 minutes, or until the zucchini is tender and slightly golden brown.
Remove the rolls from the oven and allow them to cool slightly before serving.
Serve the zucchini and mushroom rolls warm as an appetizer or side dish. They can also be served at room temperature. Enjoy!

Sweet potato and avocado rolls

Ingredients:

- Nori seaweed sheets
- 1 large sweet potato
- 1 ripe avocado
- Sushi rice
- Rice vinegar
- Sugar
- Salt
- Sesame seeds (optional)
- Soy sauce, for dipping

Instructions:

Cook the sushi rice according to package instructions. Once cooked, season it with a mixture of rice vinegar, sugar, and salt to taste. Allow the rice to cool to room temperature.
Peel the sweet potato and cut it into thin strips. Steam or boil the sweet potato until tender but still firm.
Peel and slice the avocado into thin strips.
Lay a sheet of nori seaweed on a bamboo sushi mat or clean surface, shiny side down.
Spread a thin layer of sushi rice evenly over the nori, leaving a small border along the top edge.
Arrange strips of sweet potato and avocado horizontally across the center of the rice.
Carefully roll up the nori and rice using the bamboo mat, applying gentle pressure to shape the roll. Seal the edge of the nori with a little water.
Once the roll is tightly formed, sprinkle sesame seeds over the top (if using).
Using a sharp knife, slice the roll into bite-sized pieces.
Serve the sweet potato and avocado rolls with soy sauce for dipping.

Enjoy your homemade sweet potato and avocado rolls! They make a healthy and satisfying snack or meal.

Cucumber and radish rolls

Ingredients:

- Nori seaweed sheets
- Sushi rice
- Rice vinegar
- Sugar
- Salt
- 1 cucumber
- Radishes
- Sesame seeds (optional)
- Soy sauce, for dipping

Instructions:

Cook the sushi rice according to package instructions. Once cooked, season it with a mixture of rice vinegar, sugar, and salt to taste. Allow the rice to cool to room temperature.
Wash and thinly slice the cucumber and radishes into long strips.
Lay a sheet of nori seaweed on a bamboo sushi mat or clean surface, shiny side down.
Spread a thin layer of sushi rice evenly over the nori, leaving a small border along the top edge.
Arrange strips of cucumber and radish horizontally across the center of the rice.
Carefully roll up the nori and rice using the bamboo mat, applying gentle pressure to shape the roll. Seal the edge of the nori with a little water.
Once the roll is tightly formed, sprinkle sesame seeds over the top (if using).
Using a sharp knife, slice the roll into bite-sized pieces.
Serve the cucumber and radish rolls with soy sauce for dipping.

These rolls are light, crunchy, and full of flavor—a perfect choice for a healthy snack or appetizer. Enjoy!

Spinach and sun-dried tomato rolls

Ingredients:

- Nori seaweed sheets
- Sushi rice
- Rice vinegar
- Sugar
- Salt
- Fresh spinach leaves
- Sun-dried tomatoes (packed in oil), drained and chopped
- Avocado (optional)
- Sesame seeds (optional)
- Soy sauce, for dipping

Instructions:

Cook the sushi rice according to package instructions. Once cooked, season it with a mixture of rice vinegar, sugar, and salt to taste. Allow the rice to cool to room temperature.

Wash the fresh spinach leaves and blanch them in boiling water for a minute or until wilted. Drain and pat them dry with paper towels.

Lay a sheet of nori seaweed on a bamboo sushi mat or clean surface, shiny side down.

Spread a thin layer of sushi rice evenly over the nori, leaving a small border along the top edge.

Arrange the blanched spinach leaves evenly across the rice.

Sprinkle chopped sun-dried tomatoes over the spinach. If desired, add slices of avocado for extra creaminess.

Carefully roll up the nori and rice using the bamboo mat, applying gentle pressure to shape the roll. Seal the edge of the nori with a little water.

Once the roll is tightly formed, sprinkle sesame seeds over the top (if using).

Using a sharp knife, slice the roll into bite-sized pieces.

Serve the spinach and sun-dried tomato rolls with soy sauce for dipping.

These rolls are packed with savory and slightly tangy flavors, making them a perfect choice for a light lunch or appetizer. Enjoy!

Watermelon and cucumber rolls

Ingredients:

- Nori seaweed sheets
- Sushi rice
- Rice vinegar
- Sugar
- Salt
- Seedless watermelon
- English cucumber
- Avocado (optional)
- Sesame seeds (optional)
- Soy sauce, for dipping

Instructions:

Cook the sushi rice according to package instructions. Once cooked, season it with a mixture of rice vinegar, sugar, and salt to taste. Allow the rice to cool to room temperature.
Cut the watermelon into thin, rectangular strips, about the same width as the nori seaweed sheets.
Cut the cucumber into thin, long strips, similar in size to the watermelon strips.
Lay a sheet of nori seaweed on a bamboo sushi mat or clean surface, shiny side down.
Spread a thin layer of sushi rice evenly over the nori, leaving a small border along the top edge.
Arrange strips of watermelon and cucumber horizontally across the center of the rice.
If desired, add slices of avocado for extra creaminess.
Carefully roll up the nori and rice using the bamboo mat, applying gentle pressure to shape the roll. Seal the edge of the nori with a little water.
Once the roll is tightly formed, sprinkle sesame seeds over the top (if using).
Using a sharp knife, slice the roll into bite-sized pieces.
Serve the watermelon and cucumber rolls with soy sauce for dipping.

These rolls are light, refreshing, and perfect for a summer snack or appetizer. Enjoy the delightful combination of sweet watermelon and crisp cucumber!

Pineapple and bell pepper rolls

Ingredients:

- Nori seaweed sheets
- Sushi rice
- Rice vinegar
- Sugar
- Salt
- Fresh pineapple
- Bell peppers (choose colorful ones for visual appeal)
- Avocado (optional)
- Sesame seeds (optional)
- Soy sauce, for dipping

Instructions:

Cook the sushi rice according to package instructions. Once cooked, season it with a mixture of rice vinegar, sugar, and salt to taste. Allow the rice to cool to room temperature.
Cut the fresh pineapple into thin, long strips, similar in size to the nori seaweed sheets.
Thinly slice the bell peppers into long strips, removing seeds and membranes.
Lay a sheet of nori seaweed on a bamboo sushi mat or clean surface, shiny side down.
Spread a thin layer of sushi rice evenly over the nori, leaving a small border along the top edge.
Arrange strips of pineapple and bell pepper horizontally across the center of the rice.
If desired, add slices of avocado for extra creaminess.
Carefully roll up the nori and rice using the bamboo mat, applying gentle pressure to shape the roll. Seal the edge of the nori with a little water.
Once the roll is tightly formed, sprinkle sesame seeds over the top (if using).
Using a sharp knife, slice the roll into bite-sized pieces.
Serve the pineapple and bell pepper rolls with soy sauce for dipping.

These rolls offer a burst of tropical sweetness from the pineapple combined with the crunchy texture and vibrant colors of the bell peppers. Enjoy this refreshing and satisfying treat!

Jicama and mango rolls

Ingredients:

- Nori seaweed sheets
- Sushi rice
- Rice vinegar
- Sugar
- Salt
- Jicama
- Ripe mango
- Avocado (optional)
- Sesame seeds (optional)
- Soy sauce, for dipping

Instructions:

Cook the sushi rice according to package instructions. Once cooked, season it with a mixture of rice vinegar, sugar, and salt to taste. Allow the rice to cool to room temperature.
Peel the jicama and cut it into thin, long strips, similar in size to the nori seaweed sheets.
Peel the mango and cut it into thin, long strips as well.
Lay a sheet of nori seaweed on a bamboo sushi mat or clean surface, shiny side down.
Spread a thin layer of sushi rice evenly over the nori, leaving a small border along the top edge.
Arrange strips of jicama and mango horizontally across the center of the rice.
If desired, add slices of avocado for extra creaminess.
Carefully roll up the nori and rice using the bamboo mat, applying gentle pressure to shape the roll. Seal the edge of the nori with a little water.
Once the roll is tightly formed, sprinkle sesame seeds over the top (if using).
Using a sharp knife, slice the roll into bite-sized pieces.
Serve the jicama and mango rolls with soy sauce for dipping.

These rolls offer a refreshing combination of flavors and textures, with the crunchy jicama contrasting beautifully with the sweet and juicy mango. Enjoy this delightful and healthy snack or appetizer!

Coconut and avocado rolls

Ingredients:

- Nori seaweed sheets
- Sushi rice
- Rice vinegar
- Sugar
- Salt
- Ripe avocados
- Unsweetened shredded coconut
- Avocado (optional)
- Sesame seeds (optional)
- Soy sauce, for dipping

Instructions:

Cook the sushi rice according to package instructions. Once cooked, season it with a mixture of rice vinegar, sugar, and salt to taste. Allow the rice to cool to room temperature.
Peel and slice the avocados into thin, long strips.
Lay a sheet of nori seaweed on a bamboo sushi mat or clean surface, shiny side down.
Spread a thin layer of sushi rice evenly over the nori, leaving a small border along the top edge.
Sprinkle a layer of shredded coconut evenly over the rice, covering it entirely.
Arrange strips of avocado horizontally across the center of the rice.
If desired, add slices of avocado for extra creaminess.
Carefully roll up the nori and rice using the bamboo mat, applying gentle pressure to shape the roll. Seal the edge of the nori with a little water.
Once the roll is tightly formed, sprinkle sesame seeds over the top (if using).
Using a sharp knife, slice the roll into bite-sized pieces.
Serve the coconut and avocado rolls with soy sauce for dipping.

These rolls offer a creamy texture from the avocado complemented by the tropical sweetness of coconut, creating a delightful combination. Enjoy this unique and delicious sushi roll!

Portobello mushroom and spinach rolls

Ingredients:

- Nori seaweed sheets
- Sushi rice
- Rice vinegar
- Sugar
- Salt
- Portobello mushrooms
- Fresh spinach leaves
- Soy sauce or tamari, for marinating
- Olive oil
- Garlic cloves, minced
- Sesame seeds (optional)
- Soy sauce, for dipping

Instructions:

Cook the sushi rice according to package instructions. Once cooked, season it with a mixture of rice vinegar, sugar, and salt to taste. Allow the rice to cool to room temperature.
Clean the Portobello mushrooms and remove the stems. Slice them into thin strips.
In a bowl, combine soy sauce or tamari with minced garlic. Marinate the Portobello mushroom strips in this mixture for about 15-20 minutes.
Heat a little olive oil in a pan over medium heat. Sauté the marinated mushrooms until they are tender and cooked through, about 5-7 minutes. Set aside.
Wash the fresh spinach leaves and blanch them in boiling water for a minute or until wilted. Drain and pat them dry with paper towels.
Lay a sheet of nori seaweed on a bamboo sushi mat or clean surface, shiny side down.
Spread a thin layer of sushi rice evenly over the nori, leaving a small border along the top edge.
Arrange the sautéed Portobello mushroom strips and blanched spinach leaves horizontally across the center of the rice.
Carefully roll up the nori and rice using the bamboo mat, applying gentle pressure to shape the roll. Seal the edge of the nori with a little water.
Once the roll is tightly formed, sprinkle sesame seeds over the top (if using).

Using a sharp knife, slice the roll into bite-sized pieces.
Serve the Portobello mushroom and spinach rolls with soy sauce for dipping.

These rolls offer a delicious umami flavor from the Portobello mushrooms and a nutritious boost from the spinach. Enjoy this vegetarian sushi option!

Bell pepper and avocado rolls

Ingredients:

- Nori seaweed sheets
- Sushi rice
- Rice vinegar
- Sugar
- Salt
- Ripe avocados
- Bell peppers (choose colorful ones for visual appeal)
- Sesame seeds (optional)
- Soy sauce, for dipping

Instructions:

Cook the sushi rice according to package instructions. Once cooked, season it with a mixture of rice vinegar, sugar, and salt to taste. Allow the rice to cool to room temperature.
Slice the bell peppers into thin, long strips, removing seeds and membranes.
Peel and slice the avocados into thin, long strips.
Lay a sheet of nori seaweed on a bamboo sushi mat or clean surface, shiny side down.
Spread a thin layer of sushi rice evenly over the nori, leaving a small border along the top edge.
Arrange strips of bell peppers and avocado horizontally across the center of the rice.
Carefully roll up the nori and rice using the bamboo mat, applying gentle pressure to shape the roll. Seal the edge of the nori with a little water.
Once the roll is tightly formed, sprinkle sesame seeds over the top (if using).
Using a sharp knife, slice the roll into bite-sized pieces.
Serve the bell pepper and avocado rolls with soy sauce for dipping.

These rolls offer a wonderful combination of textures and flavors, with the creamy avocado complementing the crunchy bell peppers perfectly. Enjoy this healthy and delicious sushi option!

Sweet potato and kale rolls

Ingredients:

- Nori seaweed sheets
- Sushi rice
- Rice vinegar
- Sugar
- Salt
- Sweet potatoes
- Kale leaves
- Soy sauce or tamari, for dipping

Instructions:

Cook the sushi rice according to package instructions. Once cooked, season it with a mixture of rice vinegar, sugar, and salt to taste. Allow the rice to cool to room temperature.

Peel the sweet potatoes and cut them into thin, long strips.

Wash the kale leaves thoroughly and remove the tough stems. Blanch the kale leaves in boiling water for a minute or until wilted. Drain and pat dry with paper towels.

Lay a sheet of nori seaweed on a bamboo sushi mat or clean surface, shiny side down.

Spread a thin layer of sushi rice evenly over the nori, leaving a small border along the top edge.

Arrange strips of sweet potato and kale horizontally across the center of the rice.

Carefully roll up the nori and rice using the bamboo mat, applying gentle pressure to shape the roll. Seal the edge of the nori with a little water.

Using a sharp knife, slice the roll into bite-sized pieces.

Serve the sweet potato and kale rolls with soy sauce or tamari for dipping.

These rolls offer a nutritious and satisfying option for sushi lovers, with the sweetness of the sweet potatoes complementing the earthy flavor of the kale. Enjoy this healthy and delicious dish!

Cauliflower rice and avocado rolls

Ingredients:

- Nori seaweed sheets
- Cauliflower
- Ripe avocados
- Rice vinegar
- Sugar
- Salt
- Soy sauce or tamari, for dipping

Instructions:

Prepare the cauliflower rice by pulsing cauliflower florets in a food processor until they resemble rice grains. Alternatively, you can grate the cauliflower using a box grater.
Cook the cauliflower rice in a skillet over medium heat, stirring frequently, until it's tender but not mushy. Set aside to cool.
Peel and slice the avocados into thin, long strips.
Lay a sheet of nori seaweed on a bamboo sushi mat or clean surface, shiny side down.
Spread a thin layer of cauliflower rice evenly over the nori, leaving a small border along the top edge.
Arrange strips of avocado horizontally across the center of the cauliflower rice.
Roll up the nori and cauliflower rice using the bamboo mat, applying gentle pressure to shape the roll. Seal the edge of the nori with a little water.
Using a sharp knife, slice the roll into bite-sized pieces.
Serve the cauliflower rice and avocado rolls with soy sauce or tamari for dipping.

These rolls offer a light and refreshing option for sushi lovers, with the creamy avocado complementing the texture of the cauliflower rice perfectly. Enjoy this healthy and delicious dish!

Sunflower seed pate and cucumber rolls

Ingredients:

For the Sunflower Seed Pâté:

- 1 cup raw sunflower seeds
- 2 tablespoons lemon juice
- 2 tablespoons olive oil
- 2 cloves garlic, minced
- 1 tablespoon nutritional yeast (optional)
- Salt and pepper to taste
- Water (as needed for consistency)

For the Rolls:

- Large English cucumbers
- Sunflower seed pâté
- Fresh herbs (such as cilantro, parsley, or basil), optional
- Soy sauce or tamari, for dipping

Instructions:

Prepare the Sunflower Seed Pâté:
- Soak the raw sunflower seeds in water for at least 4 hours or overnight. Drain and rinse the soaked seeds.
- In a food processor, combine the soaked sunflower seeds, lemon juice, olive oil, minced garlic, nutritional yeast (if using), salt, and pepper.
- Process the mixture until smooth, adding water as needed to achieve your desired consistency. Taste and adjust seasonings as needed.

Prepare the Rolls:
- Peel the cucumbers if desired, or leave the skin on for added texture and color. Using a vegetable peeler or a mandoline slicer, slice the cucumbers lengthwise into thin strips.
- Lay a cucumber strip flat on a clean surface. Spoon a small amount of sunflower seed pâté onto one end of the cucumber strip.
- If using fresh herbs, place a few leaves on top of the pâté.
- Carefully roll up the cucumber strip, enclosing the pâté and herbs inside. Repeat with the remaining cucumber strips and pâté.

Arrange the rolls on a serving platter and serve with soy sauce or tamari for dipping.

These sunflower seed pâté and cucumber rolls make for a light and refreshing appetizer or snack. They're perfect for those looking for a raw, vegan, or gluten-free option. Enjoy!

Kimchi and avocado rolls

Ingredients:

- Nori seaweed sheets
- Sushi rice
- Rice vinegar
- Sugar
- Salt
- Ripe avocados
- Kimchi
- Sesame seeds (optional)
- Soy sauce or tamari, for dipping

Instructions:

Cook the sushi rice according to package instructions. Once cooked, season it with a mixture of rice vinegar, sugar, and salt to taste. Allow the rice to cool to room temperature.
Peel and slice the avocados into thin, long strips.
Lay a sheet of nori seaweed on a bamboo sushi mat or clean surface, shiny side down.
Spread a thin layer of sushi rice evenly over the nori, leaving a small border along the top edge.
Arrange strips of avocado and kimchi horizontally across the center of the rice.
Carefully roll up the nori and rice using the bamboo mat, applying gentle pressure to shape the roll. Seal the edge of the nori with a little water.
Once the roll is tightly formed, sprinkle sesame seeds over the top (if using).
Using a sharp knife, slice the roll into bite-sized pieces.
Serve the kimchi and avocado rolls with soy sauce or tamari for dipping.

These rolls offer a delightful combination of creamy avocado and tangy, spicy kimchi, creating a unique and flavorful sushi experience. Enjoy this delicious fusion dish!

Nori-wrapped vegetable sticks with almond butter

Ingredients:

- Nori seaweed sheets
- Assorted vegetables (carrots, cucumber, bell peppers, etc.)
- Almond butter (or any nut or seed butter of your choice)
- Sesame seeds (optional)
- Soy sauce or tamari, for dipping

Instructions:

Wash and peel the vegetables (if desired). Cut them into thin, long sticks, suitable for wrapping.
Lay a sheet of nori seaweed on a clean surface.
Spread a thin layer of almond butter along one edge of the nori sheet.
Place the vegetable sticks horizontally across the almond butter, leaving some space at the edges.
Carefully roll up the nori sheet, enclosing the vegetable sticks and almond butter inside. Seal the edge with a little water if necessary.
Once rolled, sprinkle sesame seeds over the top (if using).
Using a sharp knife, slice the roll into bite-sized pieces.
Serve the nori-wrapped vegetable sticks with soy sauce or tamari for dipping.

These nori-wrapped vegetable sticks with almond butter offer a satisfying crunch from the vegetables, paired with the creamy richness of almond butter and the umami flavor of nori. They're a delicious and nutritious snack that's sure to please!

Cucumber and quinoa rolls

Ingredients:

- Nori seaweed sheets
- Sushi rice
- Quinoa
- Rice vinegar
- Sugar
- Salt
- English cucumbers
- Avocado (optional)
- Soy sauce or tamari, for dipping

Instructions:

Cook the sushi rice and quinoa separately according to package instructions. Once cooked, season the rice with a mixture of rice vinegar, sugar, and salt to taste. Allow both the rice and quinoa to cool to room temperature.
Peel the cucumbers if desired, or leave the skin on for added texture and color. Using a vegetable peeler or a mandoline slicer, slice the cucumbers lengthwise into thin strips.
Lay a sheet of nori seaweed on a clean surface, shiny side down.
Spread a thin layer of sushi rice evenly over the nori, leaving a small border along the top edge.
Spread a thin layer of cooked quinoa evenly over the rice.
Arrange cucumber strips horizontally across the center of the rice and quinoa.
If using avocado, slice it into thin strips and add them alongside the cucumber.
Carefully roll up the nori and rice using your hands or a bamboo sushi mat, applying gentle pressure to shape the roll. Seal the edge of the nori with a little water if necessary.
Using a sharp knife, slice the roll into bite-sized pieces.
Serve the cucumber and quinoa rolls with soy sauce or tamari for dipping.

These rolls offer a delightful combination of textures and flavors, with the refreshing crunch of cucumber and the nutty richness of quinoa. They're a healthy and satisfying option for sushi lovers. Enjoy!

Tomato and basil rolls

Ingredients:

- Nori seaweed sheets
- Sushi rice
- Rice vinegar
- Sugar
- Salt
- Ripe tomatoes
- Fresh basil leaves
- Avocado (optional)
- Soy sauce or tamari, for dipping

Instructions:

Cook the sushi rice according to package instructions. Once cooked, season it with a mixture of rice vinegar, sugar, and salt to taste. Allow the rice to cool to room temperature.
Slice the tomatoes into thin, long strips. Remove excess moisture by patting them gently with paper towels.
Wash the fresh basil leaves and pat them dry with paper towels.
Lay a sheet of nori seaweed on a clean surface, shiny side down.
Spread a thin layer of sushi rice evenly over the nori, leaving a small border along the top edge.
Arrange strips of tomato and basil leaves horizontally across the center of the rice.
If using avocado, slice it into thin strips and add them alongside the tomato and basil.
Carefully roll up the nori and rice using your hands or a bamboo sushi mat, applying gentle pressure to shape the roll. Seal the edge of the nori with a little water if necessary.
Using a sharp knife, slice the roll into bite-sized pieces.
Serve the tomato and basil rolls with soy sauce or tamari for dipping.

These rolls offer a burst of fresh flavors from the ripe tomatoes and aromatic basil, making them a delightful and light option for sushi enthusiasts. Enjoy this refreshing dish!

Broccoli and carrot rolls

Ingredients:

- Nori seaweed sheets
- Sushi rice
- Rice vinegar
- Sugar
- Salt
- Broccoli florets
- Carrots
- Avocado (optional)
- Soy sauce or tamari, for dipping

Instructions:

Cook the sushi rice according to package instructions. Once cooked, season it with a mixture of rice vinegar, sugar, and salt to taste. Allow the rice to cool to room temperature.

Steam or blanch the broccoli florets until they are tender but still crisp. Drain and set aside to cool.

Peel the carrots and cut them into thin, long strips.

Lay a sheet of nori seaweed on a clean surface, shiny side down.

Spread a thin layer of sushi rice evenly over the nori, leaving a small border along the top edge.

Arrange strips of broccoli and carrot horizontally across the center of the rice.

If using avocado, slice it into thin strips and add them alongside the broccoli and carrot.

Carefully roll up the nori and rice using your hands or a bamboo sushi mat, applying gentle pressure to shape the roll. Seal the edge of the nori with a little water if necessary.

Using a sharp knife, slice the roll into bite-sized pieces.

Serve the broccoli and carrot rolls with soy sauce or tamari for dipping.

These rolls offer a satisfying crunch from the broccoli and carrot, along with the creaminess of avocado if added, making them a delicious and healthy option for sushi lovers. Enjoy this flavorful dish!

Radish and avocado rolls

Ingredients:

- Nori seaweed sheets
- Sushi rice
- Rice vinegar
- Sugar
- Salt
- Radishes
- Ripe avocados
- Soy sauce or tamari, for dipping

Instructions:

Cook the sushi rice according to package instructions. Once cooked, season it with a mixture of rice vinegar, sugar, and salt to taste. Allow the rice to cool to room temperature.
Wash and thinly slice the radishes into long, thin strips.
Peel and slice the avocados into thin, long strips.
Lay a sheet of nori seaweed on a clean surface, shiny side down.
Spread a thin layer of sushi rice evenly over the nori, leaving a small border along the top edge.
Arrange strips of radish and avocado horizontally across the center of the rice.
Carefully roll up the nori and rice using your hands or a bamboo sushi mat, applying gentle pressure to shape the roll. Seal the edge of the nori with a little water if necessary.
Using a sharp knife, slice the roll into bite-sized pieces.
Serve the radish and avocado rolls with soy sauce or tamari for dipping.

These rolls offer a delightful contrast of textures and flavors, with the crispness of radish complementing the creaminess of avocado perfectly. Enjoy this refreshing and nutritious sushi option!

Mango and jalapeño rolls

Ingredients:

- Nori seaweed sheets
- Sushi rice
- Rice vinegar
- Sugar
- Salt
- Ripe mangoes
- Fresh jalapeño peppers
- Avocado (optional)
- Soy sauce or tamari, for dipping

Instructions:

Cook the sushi rice according to package instructions. Once cooked, season it with a mixture of rice vinegar, sugar, and salt to taste. Allow the rice to cool to room temperature.
Peel the mangoes and cut them into thin, long strips.
Slice the jalapeño peppers into thin rounds, removing the seeds if you prefer less heat.
If using avocado, peel and slice it into thin strips.
Lay a sheet of nori seaweed on a clean surface, shiny side down.
Spread a thin layer of sushi rice evenly over the nori, leaving a small border along the top edge.
Arrange strips of mango and slices of jalapeño (and avocado, if using) horizontally across the center of the rice.
Carefully roll up the nori and rice using your hands or a bamboo sushi mat, applying gentle pressure to shape the roll. Seal the edge of the nori with a little water if necessary.
Using a sharp knife, slice the roll into bite-sized pieces.
Serve the mango and jalapeño rolls with soy sauce or tamari for dipping.

These rolls offer a unique combination of sweet mango and spicy jalapeño, creating a flavor explosion in every bite. Enjoy this delicious and adventurous sushi option!

Asparagus and avocado rolls

Ingredients:

- Nori seaweed sheets
- Sushi rice
- Rice vinegar
- Sugar
- Salt
- Fresh asparagus spears
- Ripe avocados
- Soy sauce or tamari, for dipping

Instructions:

Cook the sushi rice according to package instructions. Once cooked, season it with a mixture of rice vinegar, sugar, and salt to taste. Allow the rice to cool to room temperature.

Trim the tough ends off the asparagus spears and blanch them in boiling water for about 2-3 minutes, until they are tender but still crisp. Remove them from the boiling water and immediately transfer them to a bowl of ice water to stop the cooking process. Drain and pat dry with paper towels.

Peel and slice the avocados into thin, long strips.

Lay a sheet of nori seaweed on a clean surface, shiny side down.

Spread a thin layer of sushi rice evenly over the nori, leaving a small border along the top edge.

Arrange strips of avocado and asparagus horizontally across the center of the rice.

Carefully roll up the nori and rice using your hands or a bamboo sushi mat, applying gentle pressure to shape the roll. Seal the edge of the nori with a little water if necessary.

Using a sharp knife, slice the roll into bite-sized pieces.

Serve the asparagus and avocado rolls with soy sauce or tamari for dipping.

These rolls offer a delightful combination of creamy avocado and tender-crisp asparagus, making them a delicious and satisfying sushi option. Enjoy!

Bell pepper and jicama rolls

Ingredients:

- Nori seaweed sheets
- Sushi rice
- Rice vinegar
- Sugar
- Salt
- Bell peppers (assorted colors for visual appeal)
- Jicama
- Avocado (optional)
- Soy sauce or tamari, for dipping

Instructions:

Cook the sushi rice according to the package instructions. Once cooked, season the rice with a mixture of rice vinegar, sugar, and salt to taste. Allow the rice to cool to room temperature.
Peel the jicama and cut it into thin, long strips.
Wash the bell peppers and remove the seeds and membranes. Slice them into thin, long strips.
Lay a sheet of nori seaweed on a clean surface, shiny side down.
Spread a thin layer of sushi rice evenly over the nori, leaving a small border along the top edge.
Arrange strips of bell pepper and jicama horizontally across the center of the rice.
If using avocado, slice it into thin strips and add them alongside the bell pepper and jicama.
Carefully roll up the nori and rice using your hands or a bamboo sushi mat, applying gentle pressure to shape the roll. Seal the edge of the nori with a little water if necessary.
Using a sharp knife, slice the roll into bite-sized pieces.
Serve the bell pepper and jicama rolls with soy sauce or tamari for dipping.

These rolls offer a refreshing crunch from the bell peppers and jicama, balanced with the creamy texture of avocado if included. They make for a delightful and healthy sushi option. Enjoy!

Spinach and avocado rolls

Ingredients:

- Nori seaweed sheets
- Sushi rice
- Rice vinegar
- Sugar
- Salt
- Fresh spinach leaves
- Ripe avocados
- Soy sauce or tamari, for dipping

Instructions:

Cook the sushi rice according to package instructions. Once cooked, season it with a mixture of rice vinegar, sugar, and salt to taste. Allow the rice to cool to room temperature.
Wash the fresh spinach leaves and blanch them in boiling water for about 1 minute or until wilted. Drain the spinach and immediately transfer it to a bowl of ice water to stop the cooking process. Once cooled, drain the spinach thoroughly and pat it dry with paper towels.
Peel and slice the avocados into thin, long strips.
Lay a sheet of nori seaweed on a clean surface, shiny side down.
Spread a thin layer of sushi rice evenly over the nori, leaving a small border along the top edge.
Arrange the blanched spinach leaves and avocado slices horizontally across the center of the rice.
Carefully roll up the nori and rice using your hands or a bamboo sushi mat, applying gentle pressure to shape the roll. Seal the edge of the nori with a little water if necessary.
Using a sharp knife, slice the roll into bite-sized pieces.
Serve the spinach and avocado rolls with soy sauce or tamari for dipping.

These rolls offer a wonderful combination of creamy avocado and tender spinach, making them a delicious and healthy sushi option. Enjoy!

Cabbage and carrot rolls

Ingredients:

- Nori seaweed sheets
- Sushi rice
- Rice vinegar
- Sugar
- Salt
- Green cabbage leaves
- Carrots
- Avocado (optional)
- Soy sauce or tamari, for dipping

Instructions:

Cook the sushi rice according to package instructions. Once cooked, season it with a mixture of rice vinegar, sugar, and salt to taste. Allow the rice to cool to room temperature.
Wash the cabbage leaves and pat them dry with paper towels. Carefully remove the thick stem from each cabbage leaf, ensuring the leaves remain intact.
Peel the carrots and cut them into thin, long strips.
Lay a sheet of nori seaweed on a clean surface, shiny side down.
Spread a thin layer of sushi rice evenly over the nori, leaving a small border along the top edge.
Place a cabbage leaf on top of the rice, with the edge of the leaf aligned with the top edge of the nori.
Arrange strips of carrot horizontally across the center of the cabbage leaf.
If using avocado, slice it into thin strips and add them alongside the carrot.
Carefully roll up the nori, rice, and cabbage leaf using your hands or a bamboo sushi mat, applying gentle pressure to shape the roll. Seal the edge of the nori with a little water if necessary.
Using a sharp knife, slice the roll into bite-sized pieces.
Serve the cabbage and carrot rolls with soy sauce or tamari for dipping.

These rolls offer a delightful crunch from the cabbage and carrot, and the optional addition of avocado provides a creamy texture. They're a tasty and nutritious sushi option that's perfect for a light meal or snack. Enjoy!

Sesame marinated tofu rolls

Ingredients:

For the Sesame Marinated Tofu:

- 1 block extra-firm tofu
- 2 tablespoons soy sauce or tamari
- 1 tablespoon sesame oil
- 1 tablespoon rice vinegar
- 1 teaspoon maple syrup or honey
- 1 clove garlic, minced
- 1 teaspoon grated ginger
- 1 tablespoon sesame seeds

For the Rolls:

- Nori seaweed sheets
- Sushi rice
- Rice vinegar
- Sugar
- Salt
- Cucumber, avocado, carrot, or any other desired fillings
- Soy sauce or tamari, for dipping

Instructions:

Press the tofu to remove excess water. Slice the tofu into thin strips or cubes. In a bowl, whisk together soy sauce, sesame oil, rice vinegar, maple syrup or honey, minced garlic, grated ginger, and sesame seeds to make the marinade. Place the tofu slices or cubes in the marinade and let them marinate for at least 30 minutes, or longer if possible, to allow the flavors to infuse.
While the tofu is marinating, prepare the sushi rice according to package instructions. Once cooked, season it with a mixture of rice vinegar, sugar, and salt to taste. Allow the rice to cool to room temperature.
Lay a sheet of nori seaweed on a clean surface, shiny side down.
Spread a thin layer of sushi rice evenly over the nori, leaving a small border along the top edge.

Arrange strips of marinated tofu and any desired fillings (such as cucumber, avocado, or carrot) horizontally across the center of the rice.

Carefully roll up the nori and rice using your hands or a bamboo sushi mat, applying gentle pressure to shape the roll. Seal the edge of the nori with a little water if necessary.

Using a sharp knife, slice the roll into bite-sized pieces.

Serve the sesame marinated tofu rolls with soy sauce or tamari for dipping.

These rolls offer a deliciously savory flavor from the sesame-marinated tofu, complemented by the fresh and crunchy vegetables. They're a nutritious and satisfying sushi option for vegetarians and tofu lovers alike. Enjoy!

Smoked tofu and cucumber rolls

Ingredients:

- 1 block of smoked tofu
- 1 large cucumber
- 1/4 cup of soy sauce
- 1 tablespoon of rice vinegar
- 1 teaspoon of sesame oil
- 1 teaspoon of grated ginger
- 1 teaspoon of honey or maple syrup (optional)
- Sesame seeds for garnish (optional)
- Thinly sliced green onions for garnish (optional)

Instructions:

Slice the smoked tofu into thin strips, about 1/4 inch thick.

Peel the cucumber and slice it lengthwise into thin strips using a vegetable peeler or a mandoline slicer.

In a small bowl, mix together the soy sauce, rice vinegar, sesame oil, grated ginger, and honey or maple syrup (if using). This will be your dipping sauce.

Lay a slice of cucumber flat on a cutting board. Place a strip of smoked tofu on top of the cucumber slice.

Carefully roll up the cucumber slice with the tofu inside. Repeat with the remaining cucumber slices and tofu strips.

Arrange the rolls on a serving platter and sprinkle with sesame seeds and sliced green onions, if desired.

Serve the rolls with the dipping sauce on the side.

These smoked tofu and cucumber rolls are not only tasty but also healthy and vegan-friendly. Enjoy!

Pickled ginger and avocado rolls

Ingredients:

- Sushi nori sheets
- Cooked sushi rice
- Ripe avocados, thinly sliced
- Pickled ginger slices
- Soy sauce, for dipping
- Wasabi paste (optional)

Instructions:

Lay a sushi nori sheet shiny side down on a clean surface or sushi rolling mat. Spread a thin layer of cooked sushi rice evenly over the nori sheet, leaving about 1 inch of the nori sheet uncovered at the top edge.

Place avocado slices and pickled ginger slices horizontally across the center of the rice-covered nori sheet.

Carefully lift the bottom edge of the nori sheet and begin rolling it over the filling, using your fingers to keep the filling in place.

Continue rolling until you reach the uncovered edge of the nori sheet. Wet the uncovered edge lightly with water to seal the roll.

Using a sharp knife, slice the roll into individual pieces, about 1 inch thick.

Repeat the process with the remaining nori sheets and filling ingredients.

Serve the pickled ginger and avocado rolls with soy sauce for dipping. Optionally, serve with wasabi paste on the side for extra flavor.

These rolls are not only delicious but also customizable and perfect for sushi lovers.

Enjoy!

Spicy cashew cheese and bell pepper rolls

Ingredients:

- 1 cup raw cashews, soaked in water for at least 4 hours or overnight
- 1 red bell pepper, thinly sliced
- 1 yellow bell pepper, thinly sliced
- 1 green bell pepper, thinly sliced
- 2-3 tablespoons nutritional yeast
- 1-2 cloves garlic, minced
- 1 tablespoon lemon juice
- 1/2 teaspoon chili powder
- Salt and pepper to taste
- Sushi nori sheets

Instructions:

Drain the soaked cashews and rinse them under cold water. Place them in a food processor or high-speed blender.

Add nutritional yeast, minced garlic, lemon juice, chili powder, salt, and pepper to the cashews.

Blend the mixture until smooth and creamy, adding a little water if necessary to achieve your desired consistency. Taste and adjust seasoning as needed.

Lay a sushi nori sheet shiny side down on a clean surface or sushi rolling mat.

Spread a thin layer of the spicy cashew cheese evenly over the nori sheet, leaving about 1 inch of the nori sheet uncovered at the top edge.

Place thinly sliced bell pepper strips horizontally across the center of the cashew cheese-covered nori sheet.

Carefully lift the bottom edge of the nori sheet and begin rolling it over the filling, using your fingers to keep the filling in place.

Continue rolling until you reach the uncovered edge of the nori sheet. Wet the uncovered edge lightly with water to seal the roll.

Using a sharp knife, slice the roll into individual pieces, about 1 inch thick.

Repeat the process with the remaining nori sheets and filling ingredients.

Serve the spicy cashew cheese and bell pepper rolls as is or with your favorite dipping sauce.

These rolls are not only delicious but also vegan, gluten-free, and packed with nutrients.

Enjoy!

Lentil and carrot rolls

Ingredients:

- 1 cup cooked lentils (any variety)
- 1 large carrot, grated
- 2-3 tablespoons chopped fresh parsley
- 1 tablespoon olive oil
- 1 teaspoon ground cumin
- 1/2 teaspoon ground coriander
- Salt and pepper to taste
- Sushi nori sheets
- Optional: Avocado slices, cucumber strips, or any other desired fillings

Instructions:

In a mixing bowl, combine the cooked lentils, grated carrot, chopped parsley, olive oil, ground cumin, ground coriander, salt, and pepper. Mix well to combine all the ingredients.
Lay a sushi nori sheet shiny side down on a clean surface or sushi rolling mat. Spread a thin layer of the lentil and carrot mixture evenly over the nori sheet, leaving about 1 inch of the nori sheet uncovered at the top edge.
If desired, add additional fillings such as avocado slices or cucumber strips on top of the lentil and carrot mixture.
Carefully lift the bottom edge of the nori sheet and begin rolling it over the filling, using your fingers to keep the filling in place.
Continue rolling until you reach the uncovered edge of the nori sheet. Wet the uncovered edge lightly with water to seal the roll.
Using a sharp knife, slice the roll into individual pieces, about 1 inch thick.
Repeat the process with the remaining nori sheets and filling ingredients.
Serve the lentil and carrot rolls as is or with your favorite dipping sauce.

These rolls are not only delicious but also vegan, gluten-free, and packed with protein and fiber from the lentils and carrots. Enjoy!

Kimchi and cauliflower rice rolls

Ingredients:

- Sushi nori sheets
- 2 cups cauliflower rice (homemade or store-bought)
- 1 cup kimchi, chopped
- 1 tablespoon sesame oil
- Soy sauce, for dipping (optional)
- Pickled ginger and wasabi, for serving (optional)

Instructions:

If you're using homemade cauliflower rice, grate or process cauliflower florets until they resemble rice grains. If using store-bought cauliflower rice, measure out 2 cups.

Heat sesame oil in a skillet over medium heat. Add the cauliflower rice and sauté for 5-7 minutes, or until tender.

Remove the skillet from heat and let the cauliflower rice cool slightly.

Lay a sushi nori sheet shiny side down on a clean surface or sushi rolling mat.

Spread a thin layer of cauliflower rice evenly over the nori sheet, leaving about 1 inch of the nori sheet uncovered at the top edge.

Spread a layer of chopped kimchi over the cauliflower rice.

Carefully lift the bottom edge of the nori sheet and begin rolling it over the filling, using your fingers to keep the filling in place.

Continue rolling until you reach the uncovered edge of the nori sheet. Wet the uncovered edge lightly with water to seal the roll.

Using a sharp knife, slice the roll into individual pieces, about 1 inch thick.

Repeat the process with the remaining nori sheets and filling ingredients.

Serve the kimchi and cauliflower rice rolls with soy sauce for dipping, and optionally, pickled ginger and wasabi on the side.

These rolls are not only tasty but also low in carbs and packed with flavor from the kimchi. Enjoy this unique sushi variation!

Beet and spinach rolls

Ingredients:

- Sushi nori sheets
- 1 large beet, cooked, peeled, and thinly sliced
- 2 cups fresh spinach leaves
- 1 cup cooked sushi rice
- Rice vinegar (for seasoning the rice)
- Soy sauce or tamari, for dipping
- Pickled ginger and wasabi, for serving (optional)

Instructions:

Cook sushi rice according to package instructions. Once cooked, let it cool slightly. Season the rice with a splash of rice vinegar and mix well.
Lay a sushi nori sheet shiny side down on a clean surface or sushi rolling mat. Spread a thin layer of cooked sushi rice evenly over the nori sheet, leaving about 1 inch of the nori sheet uncovered at the top edge.
Arrange thinly sliced beet and fresh spinach leaves horizontally across the center of the rice-covered nori sheet.
Carefully lift the bottom edge of the nori sheet and begin rolling it over the filling, using your fingers to keep the filling in place.
Continue rolling until you reach the uncovered edge of the nori sheet. Wet the uncovered edge lightly with water to seal the roll.
Using a sharp knife, slice the roll into individual pieces, about 1 inch thick.
Repeat the process with the remaining nori sheets and filling ingredients.
Serve the beet and spinach rolls with soy sauce or tamari for dipping, and optionally, pickled ginger and wasabi on the side.

These rolls are not only visually appealing but also nutritious and delicious. Enjoy this colorful twist on sushi!

Cucumber and mango rolls

Ingredients:

- Sushi nori sheets
- Cooked sushi rice
- 1 ripe mango, thinly sliced
- 1 cucumber, thinly sliced
- Optional: Avocado slices, pickled ginger, or toasted sesame seeds for garnish
- Soy sauce, for dipping

Instructions:

Lay a sushi nori sheet shiny side down on a clean surface or sushi rolling mat.

Spread a thin layer of cooked sushi rice evenly over the nori sheet, leaving about 1 inch of the nori sheet uncovered at the top edge.

Arrange thinly sliced mango and cucumber strips horizontally across the center of the rice-covered nori sheet.

If desired, add additional fillings such as avocado slices or pickled ginger on top of the mango and cucumber.

Carefully lift the bottom edge of the nori sheet and begin rolling it over the filling, using your fingers to keep the filling in place.

Continue rolling until you reach the uncovered edge of the nori sheet. Wet the uncovered edge lightly with water to seal the roll.

Using a sharp knife, slice the roll into individual pieces, about 1 inch thick.

If desired, garnish the rolls with toasted sesame seeds.

Serve the cucumber and mango rolls with soy sauce for dipping.

These rolls are not only delicious but also vegan-friendly and bursting with flavors.

Enjoy!

Cauliflower rice and avocado rolls with sesame seeds

Ingredients:

- Sushi nori sheets
- Cooked cauliflower rice (homemade or store-bought)
- Ripe avocado, thinly sliced
- Toasted sesame seeds
- Soy sauce, for dipping (optional)
- Pickled ginger and wasabi, for serving (optional)

Instructions:

Lay a sushi nori sheet shiny side down on a clean surface or sushi rolling mat. Spread a thin layer of cooked cauliflower rice evenly over the nori sheet, leaving about 1 inch of the nori sheet uncovered at the top edge.
Place thinly sliced avocado strips horizontally across the center of the cauliflower rice-covered nori sheet.
Sprinkle toasted sesame seeds over the avocado slices.
Carefully lift the bottom edge of the nori sheet and begin rolling it over the filling, using your fingers to keep the filling in place.
Continue rolling until you reach the uncovered edge of the nori sheet. Wet the uncovered edge lightly with water to seal the roll.
Using a sharp knife, slice the roll into individual pieces, about 1 inch thick.
Repeat the process with the remaining nori sheets and filling ingredients.
Serve the cauliflower rice and avocado rolls with soy sauce for dipping, and optionally, pickled ginger and wasabi on the side.

These rolls are not only delicious but also low in carbs and packed with nutrients from the cauliflower and avocado. Enjoy this healthy and flavorful sushi variation!

Red cabbage and carrot rolls

Ingredients:

- Sushi nori sheets
- Cooked sushi rice
- Red cabbage, thinly sliced
- Carrot, julienned or thinly sliced
- Rice vinegar (for seasoning rice)
- Soy sauce, for dipping
- Pickled ginger and wasabi, for serving (optional)

Instructions:

Cook sushi rice according to package instructions. Once cooked, season the rice with a splash of rice vinegar and let it cool slightly.

Lay a sushi nori sheet shiny side down on a clean surface or sushi rolling mat.

Spread a thin layer of cooked sushi rice evenly over the nori sheet, leaving about 1 inch of the nori sheet uncovered at the top edge.

Arrange thinly sliced red cabbage and julienned carrots horizontally across the center of the rice-covered nori sheet.

Carefully lift the bottom edge of the nori sheet and begin rolling it over the filling, using your fingers to keep the filling in place.

Continue rolling until you reach the uncovered edge of the nori sheet. Wet the uncovered edge lightly with water to seal the roll.

Using a sharp knife, slice the roll into individual pieces, about 1 inch thick.

Repeat the process with the remaining nori sheets and filling ingredients.

Serve the red cabbage and carrot rolls with soy sauce for dipping, and optionally, pickled ginger and wasabi on the side.

These rolls are not only vibrant and visually appealing but also packed with fiber and nutrients from the red cabbage and carrots. Enjoy this healthy and delicious snack!

Sunflower seed pate and cucumber rolls

Ingredients:

- Sushi nori sheets
- 1 large cucumber
- Sunflower seed pâté (see recipe below)
- Optional: Soy sauce or tamari, for dipping

For the Sunflower Seed Pâté:

- 1 cup raw sunflower seeds, soaked in water for at least 4 hours or overnight
- 2 tablespoons lemon juice
- 2 tablespoons nutritional yeast
- 1 clove garlic, minced
- 1 tablespoon tamari or soy sauce
- 2 tablespoons water (adjust as needed for desired consistency)
- Salt and pepper to taste

Instructions for Sunflower Seed Pâté:

Drain and rinse the soaked sunflower seeds.
In a food processor or blender, combine the sunflower seeds, lemon juice, nutritional yeast, minced garlic, tamari or soy sauce, water, salt, and pepper. Blend until smooth and creamy, scraping down the sides of the processor or blender as needed. Add more water if necessary to reach your desired consistency. Adjust seasoning to taste.

Instructions for Sunflower Seed Pâté and Cucumber Rolls:

Using a vegetable peeler or a mandoline slicer, slice the cucumber lengthwise into thin strips.
Lay a sushi nori sheet shiny side down on a clean surface or sushi rolling mat. Spread a thin layer of sunflower seed pâté evenly over the nori sheet, leaving about 1 inch of the nori sheet uncovered at the top edge.
Place cucumber strips horizontally across the center of the pâté-covered nori sheet.
Carefully lift the bottom edge of the nori sheet and begin rolling it over the filling, using your fingers to keep the filling in place.

Continue rolling until you reach the uncovered edge of the nori sheet. Wet the uncovered edge lightly with water to seal the roll.
Using a sharp knife, slice the roll into individual pieces, about 1 inch thick.
Repeat the process with the remaining nori sheets and filling ingredients.
Serve the sunflower seed pâté and cucumber rolls with soy sauce or tamari for dipping, if desired.

These rolls are not only delicious but also vegan, gluten-free, and packed with plant-based protein and nutrients. Enjoy this healthy and flavorful snack!

Portobello mushroom and avocado rolls

Ingredients:

- Sushi nori sheets
- Cooked sushi rice
- 2 large portobello mushrooms, sliced
- 1 ripe avocado, thinly sliced
- Soy sauce or tamari, for dipping
- Pickled ginger and wasabi, for serving (optional)

Instructions:

Lay a sushi nori sheet shiny side down on a clean surface or sushi rolling mat. Spread a thin layer of cooked sushi rice evenly over the nori sheet, leaving about 1 inch of the nori sheet uncovered at the top edge.
Place sliced portobello mushrooms and avocado slices horizontally across the center of the rice-covered nori sheet.
Carefully lift the bottom edge of the nori sheet and begin rolling it over the filling, using your fingers to keep the filling in place.
Continue rolling until you reach the uncovered edge of the nori sheet. Wet the uncovered edge lightly with water to seal the roll.
Using a sharp knife, slice the roll into individual pieces, about 1 inch thick.
Repeat the process with the remaining nori sheets and filling ingredients.
Serve the portobello mushroom and avocado rolls with soy sauce or tamari for dipping, and optionally, pickled ginger and wasabi on the side.

These rolls are not only delicious but also vegetarian, gluten-free, and packed with nutrients from the mushrooms and avocado. Enjoy this flavorful and satisfying snack!

Mango and red cabbage rolls

Ingredients:

- Sushi nori sheets
- Cooked sushi rice
- 1 ripe mango, thinly sliced
- Red cabbage, thinly sliced
- Rice vinegar (for seasoning rice)
- Soy sauce or tamari, for dipping
- Pickled ginger and wasabi, for serving (optional)

Instructions:

Cook sushi rice according to package instructions. Once cooked, season the rice with a splash of rice vinegar and let it cool slightly.
Lay a sushi nori sheet shiny side down on a clean surface or sushi rolling mat.
Spread a thin layer of cooked sushi rice evenly over the nori sheet, leaving about 1 inch of the nori sheet uncovered at the top edge.
Arrange thinly sliced mango and red cabbage strips horizontally across the center of the rice-covered nori sheet.
Carefully lift the bottom edge of the nori sheet and begin rolling it over the filling, using your fingers to keep the filling in place.
Continue rolling until you reach the uncovered edge of the nori sheet. Wet the uncovered edge lightly with water to seal the roll.
Using a sharp knife, slice the roll into individual pieces, about 1 inch thick.
Repeat the process with the remaining nori sheets and filling ingredients.
Serve the mango and red cabbage rolls with soy sauce or tamari for dipping, and optionally, pickled ginger and wasabi on the side.

These rolls are not only delicious but also vegan, gluten-free, and bursting with flavor and nutrients. Enjoy this vibrant and refreshing sushi variation!

Spinach and bell pepper rolls

Ingredients:

- Sushi nori sheets
- Cooked sushi rice
- Fresh spinach leaves
- Red bell pepper, thinly sliced
- Yellow bell pepper, thinly sliced
- Rice vinegar (for seasoning rice)
- Soy sauce or tamari, for dipping
- Pickled ginger and wasabi, for serving (optional)

Instructions:

Cook sushi rice according to package instructions. Once cooked, season the rice with a splash of rice vinegar and let it cool slightly.
Lay a sushi nori sheet shiny side down on a clean surface or sushi rolling mat.
Spread a thin layer of cooked sushi rice evenly over the nori sheet, leaving about 1 inch of the nori sheet uncovered at the top edge.
Place fresh spinach leaves and thinly sliced red and yellow bell peppers horizontally across the center of the rice-covered nori sheet.
Carefully lift the bottom edge of the nori sheet and begin rolling it over the filling, using your fingers to keep the filling in place.
Continue rolling until you reach the uncovered edge of the nori sheet. Wet the uncovered edge lightly with water to seal the roll.
Using a sharp knife, slice the roll into individual pieces, about 1 inch thick.
Repeat the process with the remaining nori sheets and filling ingredients.
Serve the spinach and bell pepper rolls with soy sauce or tamari for dipping, and optionally, pickled ginger and wasabi on the side.

These rolls are not only delicious but also vegetarian, vegan, and gluten-free, packed with nutrients from the spinach and bell peppers. Enjoy this healthy and colorful sushi variation!

Sweet potato and cucumber rolls

Ingredients:

- Sushi nori sheets
- Cooked sushi rice
- 1 medium sweet potato, peeled and cut into thin strips
- 1 cucumber, cut into thin strips
- Rice vinegar (for seasoning rice)
- Soy sauce or tamari, for dipping
- Pickled ginger and wasabi, for serving (optional)

Instructions:

Cook sushi rice according to package instructions. Once cooked, season the rice with a splash of rice vinegar and let it cool slightly.
Lay a sushi nori sheet shiny side down on a clean surface or sushi rolling mat.
Spread a thin layer of cooked sushi rice evenly over the nori sheet, leaving about 1 inch of the nori sheet uncovered at the top edge.
Place sweet potato strips and cucumber strips horizontally across the center of the rice-covered nori sheet.
Carefully lift the bottom edge of the nori sheet and begin rolling it over the filling, using your fingers to keep the filling in place.
Continue rolling until you reach the uncovered edge of the nori sheet. Wet the uncovered edge lightly with water to seal the roll.
Using a sharp knife, slice the roll into individual pieces, about 1 inch thick.
Repeat the process with the remaining nori sheets and filling ingredients.
Serve the sweet potato and cucumber rolls with soy sauce or tamari for dipping, and optionally, pickled ginger and wasabi on the side.

These rolls are not only delicious but also vegetarian, vegan, and gluten-free, packed with nutrients from the sweet potato and cucumber. Enjoy this healthy and flavorful sushi variation!

Beet and apple rolls

Ingredients:

- Sushi nori sheets
- Cooked sushi rice
- 1 medium beet, cooked and thinly sliced
- 1 apple, thinly sliced
- Rice vinegar (for seasoning rice)
- Soy sauce or tamari, for dipping
- Pickled ginger and wasabi, for serving (optional)

Instructions:

Cook sushi rice according to package instructions. Once cooked, season the rice with a splash of rice vinegar and let it cool slightly.
Lay a sushi nori sheet shiny side down on a clean surface or sushi rolling mat.
Spread a thin layer of cooked sushi rice evenly over the nori sheet, leaving about 1 inch of the nori sheet uncovered at the top edge.
Place thinly sliced beets and apples horizontally across the center of the rice-covered nori sheet.
Carefully lift the bottom edge of the nori sheet and begin rolling it over the filling, using your fingers to keep the filling in place.
Continue rolling until you reach the uncovered edge of the nori sheet. Wet the uncovered edge lightly with water to seal the roll.
Using a sharp knife, slice the roll into individual pieces, about 1 inch thick.
Repeat the process with the remaining nori sheets and filling ingredients.
Serve the beet and apple rolls with soy sauce or tamari for dipping, and optionally, pickled ginger and wasabi on the side.

These rolls are not only delicious but also vegetarian, vegan, and gluten-free, packed with nutrients from the beets and apples. Enjoy this creative and colorful sushi variation!

Mango and avocado rolls with cilantro

Ingredients:

- 1 ripe mango, peeled and sliced into thin strips
- 1 ripe avocado, peeled, pitted, and sliced into thin strips
- Fresh cilantro leaves
- Rice paper wrappers
- Warm water for soaking the rice paper wrappers
- Optional: dipping sauce (such as soy sauce, sweet chili sauce, or peanut sauce)

Instructions:

Prepare all your ingredients by slicing the mango, avocado, and gathering the cilantro leaves.
Fill a shallow dish or large bowl with warm water.
Dip one rice paper wrapper into the warm water, ensuring it's completely submerged for about 10-15 seconds until it softens.
Carefully remove the softened rice paper wrapper from the water and lay it flat on a clean surface.
Arrange a few slices of mango and avocado in the center of the rice paper wrapper, leaving some space around the edges.
Add a few cilantro leaves on top of the mango and avocado slices.
Fold the bottom edge of the rice paper wrapper over the filling, then fold in the sides, and roll tightly to form a neat roll.
Repeat the process with the remaining rice paper wrappers and filling ingredients.
Once all the rolls are assembled, you can serve them whole or slice them into bite-sized pieces for a more elegant presentation.
If desired, serve the mango and avocado rolls with your favorite dipping sauce on the side.

Enjoy your delicious mango and avocado rolls with cilantro! They're not only tasty but also visually appealing and packed with fresh flavors.

Carrot and sunflower seed pate rolls

Ingredients:

For the Carrot and Sunflower Seed Pâté:

- 2 large carrots, peeled and roughly chopped
- 1/2 cup sunflower seeds
- 2 cloves garlic, minced
- 2 tablespoons lemon juice
- 2 tablespoons olive oil
- Salt and pepper to taste
- Water (as needed for blending)

For the Rolls:

- Rice paper wrappers
- Warm water for soaking the rice paper wrappers
- Thinly sliced vegetables for filling (such as cucumber, bell pepper, lettuce, etc.)
- Fresh herbs (such as cilantro, mint, or basil)

Instructions:

For the Carrot and Sunflower Seed Pâté:

> In a blender or food processor, combine the chopped carrots, sunflower seeds, minced garlic, lemon juice, olive oil, salt, and pepper.
> Blend the ingredients until smooth, adding water gradually as needed to achieve a spreadable consistency. Adjust the seasoning to taste.

For the Rolls:

> Fill a shallow dish or large bowl with warm water.
> Dip one rice paper wrapper into the warm water, ensuring it's completely submerged for about 10-15 seconds until it softens.
> Carefully remove the softened rice paper wrapper from the water and lay it flat on a clean surface.
> Spread a layer of the carrot and sunflower seed pâté onto the center of the rice paper wrapper, leaving some space around the edges.
> Arrange thinly sliced vegetables and fresh herbs on top of the pâté.

Fold the bottom edge of the rice paper wrapper over the filling, then fold in the sides, and roll tightly to form a neat roll.

Repeat the process with the remaining rice paper wrappers and filling ingredients.

Once all the rolls are assembled, you can serve them whole or slice them into bite-sized pieces for a more elegant presentation.

Optionally, serve the rolls with a dipping sauce of your choice, such as a soy sauce-based dip or a tahini-based sauce.

These carrot and sunflower seed pâté rolls are not only delicious but also packed with nutrients and flavors. They make a wonderful addition to any meal or gathering. Enjoy!

Cucumber and marinated tofu rolls

Ingredients:

For the Marinated Tofu:

- 1 block firm tofu, pressed and sliced into thin strips
- 3 tablespoons soy sauce
- 1 tablespoon rice vinegar
- 1 tablespoon sesame oil
- 1 teaspoon grated ginger
- 1 clove garlic, minced
- 1 teaspoon honey or maple syrup (optional)

For the Rolls:

- 1 large cucumber
- Rice paper wrappers
- Warm water for soaking the rice paper wrappers
- Thinly sliced vegetables (such as bell pepper, carrot, lettuce, etc.)
- Fresh herbs (such as cilantro, mint, or basil)
- Optional: dipping sauce (such as soy sauce, sweet chili sauce, or peanut sauce)

Instructions:

For the Marinated Tofu:

In a shallow dish or bowl, whisk together the soy sauce, rice vinegar, sesame oil, grated ginger, minced garlic, and honey or maple syrup (if using).
Add the sliced tofu to the marinade, ensuring it's well coated. Let it marinate for at least 30 minutes, or longer for more flavor.

For the Rolls:

Peel the cucumber and slice it lengthwise into thin strips using a vegetable peeler or a mandoline slicer. Alternatively, you can use a spiralizer to create cucumber noodles.
Fill a shallow dish or large bowl with warm water.
Dip one rice paper wrapper into the warm water, ensuring it's completely submerged for about 10-15 seconds until it softens.
Carefully remove the softened rice paper wrapper from the water and lay it flat on a clean surface.

Arrange a few strips of marinated tofu and cucumber slices on the bottom third of the rice paper wrapper, leaving some space around the edges.

Add thinly sliced vegetables and fresh herbs on top of the tofu and cucumber.

Fold the bottom edge of the rice paper wrapper over the filling, then fold in the sides, and roll tightly to form a neat roll.

Repeat the process with the remaining rice paper wrappers and filling ingredients.

Once all the rolls are assembled, you can serve them whole or slice them into bite-sized pieces for a more elegant presentation.

Optionally, serve the rolls with a dipping sauce of your choice.

These cucumber and marinated tofu rolls are not only tasty but also packed with plant-based protein and nutrients. They make a delightful addition to any meal or gathering. Enjoy!

Avocado and bell pepper rolls

Ingredients:

- 2 ripe avocados, peeled, pitted, and sliced into thin strips
- 2 bell peppers (any color), thinly sliced
- Rice paper wrappers
- Warm water for soaking the rice paper wrappers
- Thinly sliced vegetables (such as cucumber, carrot, lettuce, etc.)
- Fresh herbs (such as cilantro, mint, or basil)
- Optional: dipping sauce (such as soy sauce, sweet chili sauce, or peanut sauce)

Instructions:

> Fill a shallow dish or large bowl with warm water.
> Dip one rice paper wrapper into the warm water, ensuring it's completely submerged for about 10-15 seconds until it softens.
> Carefully remove the softened rice paper wrapper from the water and lay it flat on a clean surface.
> Arrange a few slices of avocado and bell pepper on the bottom third of the rice paper wrapper, leaving some space around the edges.
> Add thinly sliced vegetables and fresh herbs on top of the avocado and bell pepper.
> Fold the bottom edge of the rice paper wrapper over the filling, then fold in the sides, and roll tightly to form a neat roll.
> Repeat the process with the remaining rice paper wrappers and filling ingredients.
> Once all the rolls are assembled, you can serve them whole or slice them into bite-sized pieces for a more elegant presentation.
> Optionally, serve the rolls with a dipping sauce of your choice.

These avocado and bell pepper rolls are not only delicious but also packed with

nutrients and flavors. They make a wonderful addition to any meal or gathering. Enjoy!

www.ingramcontent.com/pod-product-compliance
Lightning Source LLC
LaVergne TN
LVHW061948070526
838199LV00060B/4029